Something So Good It Can Never Be Enough

Also by Shuly Xóchitl Cawood

NONFICTION
The Going and Goodbye: A Memoir
52 Things I Wish I Could Have Told Myself When I Was 17
What the Fortune Teller Would Have Said (flash essays)

FICTION
A Small Thing to Want: Stories

POETRY
Trouble Can Be So Beautiful at the Beginning

SOMETHING SO GOOD
IT CAN NEVER
BE ENOUGH

POEMS

SHULY XÓCHITL CAWOOD

Press 53
Winston-Salem

Press 53, LLC
PO Box 30314
Winston-Salem, NC 27130

First Edition

Cover art, "Yellow and White Bokeh Lights"
Copyright © 2020 by Hatice Yardım,
licensed through Unsplash

Author photo by Melissa Porter Fast

Cover design by Shuly Xóchitl Cawood

Library of Congress Control Number
2023941569

ISBN 978-1-950413-66-9

*for my parents, Hap and Sonia,
who have always made my world a better place*

Acknowledgments

The author thanks the editors of the publications where these poems first appeared, occasionally in different form:

"But First," *Rogue Agent*, Nov 1, 2021 ("Starter Marriage" in this collection)

"Confession," *Welter*, 2021

"Grow," *Loud Coffee Press*, July 2021

"Halfway," originally published in *The Pinch*, 2021

"Hunger," *ASP Bulletin*, July 2, 2021 (selected as a winner of Alan Squire Publishing's April 2021 National Poetry Month Contest and nominated for a Pushcart Prize)

"Letter to the Children of the Future," *We Were Not Alone: a Community Building Art Works Anthology*, November 2021

"My Mother Says She Does Not Know How to Cook," *The Sun*, December 2021

"Notes on Nostalgia," *The Acentos Review,* September 2021

"OBIT: Good Girlfriend," *Pennsylvania English*, Spring 2022

"On the Day My Bridal Dress Goes to Goodwill," *The Coop: A Poetry Cooperative*, July 2021

"Places I Looked for You," *I Thought I Heard A Cardinal Sing: Ohio's Appalachian Voices*, March 2022

"Poem in Which I Fail to Teach My Dog How to Fetch," *The Sun*, August 2023

"Practicing," *One*, August 2, 2021

"Soft-Boiled Eggs on Any Morning," *Appalachian Places*, Spring 2022

"Some Kind of Prayer," *I Thought I Heard A Cardinal Sing: Ohio's Appalachian Voices*, March 2022

"The End of the Season": parts of this poem were used in "The Last Biscuit," Tiny Love Stories, *The New York Times*, May 11, 2021

"The Last Holiday Party," *Pennsylvania English*, Spring 2022

"The Road of Love," *Appalachian Places*, Spring 2022

"We Writers," *Appalachian Places*, Spring 2022

"What I Mean When I Say Agronomist," *Jelly Bucket*, 2022, nominated for a Pushcart Prize

"What It Takes," *ASP Bulletin*, July 2, 2021

"Your Story Here," *Sheila-Na-Gig online*, December 2021

Contents

Something So Good
It Can Never
Be Enough

My Mother Says She Does Not Know How to Cook

"How did you make this?" she always asks. "A recipe," I tell her. No magic trick. No skill. Just buying ingredients, following directions, not varying from what I'm supposed to do. My mother looks in her fridge and pulls out vegetables, slices them, even keeps the stems, sautés them, adds an egg, adds some rice, and what about that can of water chestnuts, that might be good, and is there a tomato in the garden? Oh, there's cilantro out there, let's add that.

When she was thirteen, she boarded a train from Mexico to the U.S. She knew no English. There were no instructions for how to become fluent, but she did, how to skip two grades or graduate at the top of her class, but she did, how to survive far from her parents, how to sleep alone instead of in the double beds she'd shared with her sisters. She did. No one told her how to measure a person by their honesty and kindness, not their good looks or money, not their empty promises, but she learned. She swears she can't cook, but my sister and I grew up eating well: beans stewed with onions and peppers and sprinkled with cheese; roasted eggplant or buttered squash or broccoli baked into dishes she concocted to make sense of the kitchen in which she found herself.

Now I cook for her: red-lentil soup with lemon, yogurt berry pie, broccoli-with-feta pasta, all from easy recipes. "You're so good at cooking," she says, even knowing how to give praise—unwarranted, in heaps, how to make everything sweet.

Halfway

for JER

You and your honey-colored hair, your round face. We sat
in a booth at Bob Evans, halfway between my one-stoplight

town and your city with its circular highways. We ate
breakfast for dinner, we talked of our futures

though they felt like past tense. Out the window, a parking lot
of stars we could not yet see. You and your slender wrists,

your thick eyebrows that a man would someday say
could write a love story. We longed for spectacular endings

but there was the black and white clock on the wall, the bill
the waitress dropped onto our table without

saying a word. I did not want to drive back
to my apartment with its dark-corner kitchen and off-kilter

fan that clunked the bathroom air. He might call, but might not—
this was always the question that got stuck in the cobwebs

and I asked you how long I should wait. Waiting was the flat
pillow on my bed, the crumbs lost in the bottom of the rusted

toaster, the doorbell that did not know anymore how to utter
a sound. You and your pale skin, your own dark troubles,

your *it's-gonna-be-okay* ways. I would see you in a few days,
each of us in black skirts that twirled on a dance floor

of forgetting. But that night and so many others
we sat at Bob Evans until ours was the only table not yet

wiped clean. We lay our forks down on our plates and slid
the salt and pepper shakers back in place. We paid whatever

price our young decisions cost. Outside, the moon
shone like a silver coin not yet spent, not yet lost.

You're Just About to Leave After Meeting This Guy
for a Drink

and then he says he wants to order nachos
and you sit there while he points to the sticky menu
and you wait for the cook in the back
or maybe not even the cook but the server himself
or maybe the busser or the dishwasher
or maybe someone back there with no culinary skills—
no ability to distinguish jalapeños from green peppers
or hothouse from homegrown tomatoes—
to scoop some chips that have likely been hanging out
under a heat lamp since last night, and they will bunch

and crowd into a plastic basket not even a real woven one
but one of those red ones with squares for holes and one that has
probably held a hundred nacho orders and a thousand greasy fries
and too many onion rings battered and dunked too deep in oil
and on top of it all will spread some kind of version of shiny cheese.

You sit and wait for it, for what he wants, for that order of nachos
to arrive and when it does you will take a chip
because he'll push them all toward the middle
and this will be the first of so many useless offerings
and you'll take another and then another
because you think it's polite when really
you won't want any of them
so over-salted and already
cold

and it will take you years
to understand
how long
this kind
of sitting
and waiting
can last

What I Mean When I Say Agronomist

after Geffrey Davis

Garden hoses snake the greenhouse floor.
The floor glistens, wet. Steam strokes windows.

I am looking for him after my desk job ends—
he has no set hours just as rain doesn't run by clocks.
I write his kind of story into press releases
but I do not know how to tame
wild things into rows.

He mixes perlite with black soil, combs his hands
through its crumbles, cool.

We have begun though we do not know this yet.

He is a man who knows how to do most things:
change oil, fix engines, debate, forecast,
grow a whole plot of land into something
we can eat.

This is the first time I have come to him
when there is no good reason to,
when the building should be locked,
when the last bus will soon be on its way.

It is May, June, or this kind of July:
with a heat so unbearable it breaks
good decisions.

I will come to him again when I am about to marry.
I will come to him again when my marriage ends.
I am learning in this late hour that finding him
at dusk, when the light is half-spent,
is my way of meting out the costs of keeping him.

He dips his hands into a black plastic pot,
mixes perlite into soil, and those little white beads
promise so much: aeration, drainage, room to breathe,
a stronger, bigger harvest.

But love, this love, is still so small.

The Weather Today

Fussy. Like a dirty
Sunday dress
tossed
in the wash. Like
a bitchfest,
a messy counter,
a crumpled paper,
like an argument
between ex-lovers
who still steal
each other's breath.

My Mother's One Request

I must have been fifteen when I made them the first time.
Too skinny and standing by the stove. I had appointed myself

family baker, and I kneaded, rolled, poured batter
and dough into shapes everyone would want.

My mother loved bread—pumpernickel loaves, cornmeal muffins,
sourdough slices. But what she wanted most

was my buttermilk rolls from a *New York Times*
Natural Foods Cookbook, and whenever she asked,

I slipped the apron over my head and tied it behind my
back and pulled out ingredients: yeast & honey;

buttermilk & butter; unbleached white flour, sea
salt, baking soda. To do it right you had to let the dough rise

twice before dividing it into twenty-four pieces and letting all of it
rise again. Rising takes the kind of time you give knowing

you won't get it back. But I was sixteen and seventeen
and did not understand these kinds of hours.

My mother stood beside me at the stove when it was over,
pinched a roll open. Steam loosened, floated free.

For years my mother asked me to make her buttermilk rolls,
and I did and then I didn't, having tired of the recipe and its need

for each long rise. But I can't tell you how often I remember
those rolls now, the way my mother savored each one,

how she wanted each trayful to yield
more than it did, and how I did not know—

had no earthly idea—that something could be so good
it could never be enough.

Starter Marriage

after Erin Adair-Hodges

First there was the word and the word was *trying*.
Trying the apartment with white walls, popcorn ceilings,
footsteps heavy above, thudding over our days.

Trying the job I took filing papers into squeaking cabinets,
the one you took answering phones for dentists. *Trying*
the brown-bag lunches with limp sandwiches

and sliced cheese, the softening apple, the room-temperature
soda. Consuming it all on church steps, hunched below
the overhang as it rained. *Trying* the cold pool after work

with dead insects needing to be netted. Unraveling towels,
TJ Maxx suits, the walk back on the no-car driveway.
All heat evaporated. Empty stomachs. No one wanted what the other craved.

Trying the red Chevrolet with the bad battery, no parking without pay,
the bus rides to and from work, your stop, my stop, the sun hitting hard,
us squinting at the sky. Your last day, the blue electric toothbrush

they gave you as goodbye. Buzzing in your mouth with all those
trapped words. *Trying* the new queen mattress
we could not afford but bought anyway.

Trying the laundry we toted to the next
building, plastic hampers in our
arms full of every day's dirt.

Coffee but no creamer,
bread but no toaster,
sugar hardened in the bag.

Day-old everything bagels,
buy-one, get-one veggie burritos,
dollar theater on Sundays.

New job but less pay, new boss
but no promotion. Saving for tickets
for never vacations.

Trying the places we gave up for each other:
city salted by an ocean, all those fish and ferry rides;
town with three stoplights, two policemen,
a forest to get lost in. Your dreams, my dreams,

weeds by the parking lot. *Trying*
your face a broken banister,
my hands an unused map.

We're Just Not That Into You

a found poem, made entirely out of rejection letters
sent to me by literary journals

I'm sorry

I'm afraid

As you know

unfortunately

we struggle

                              sorry

                                       very sorry

                        please accept our apologies

had a good discussion about it

don't have the space
could not find a place
isn't enough room

                      plenty to admire
                      much to admire

forced to pass

unable to accept

we regret

we will not

please do not interpret this

odds are always long

must decline

I am sorry I don't have better

                      we delight in
                      we appreciate

                      agreed on the wonder of
                      are grateful

didn't understand
had trouble with
needed more

not what we're looking for

Sorry to disappoint

we know we've taken a long time

                think of us
                keep us in mind

We're sad

not for us

we've assembled a list of other

                We wish you success
                we encourage you
                we wish you all the best
                thank you for trusting us
                thanks again!

                with care
                with interest and care

wish you nothing but the best

Good luck

best of luck
best of luck
best of luck

elsewhere.

Practicing

after Ciona Rouse

I drove alone from North Carolina to my Ohio hometown
for Christmases. You and I always said we would celebrate sometime
later. Those were the trips I learned to pay the toll for the car behind me

on the West Virginia Turnpike, understanding then that small joys
might be enough. One September weekend I went to Boone
with my girlfriends while you stayed back (played tennis

with your friend whose name I can't remember, went drinking
with another who liked that taquería on the outskirts of Carrboro,
the two of you taking up a vinyl booth with your politics and beer)

and my friends and I went to a bar in broad daylight
and someone convinced one of us to mount the mechanical bull
and hold on tightly, when really the trick was to have one hand free.

In November, a friend invited us to contra dance at a rec center two towns
away. You said you wouldn't like the music—fiddle and guitar—so I pulled
my hair back and went without you. Two men asked my name. One

had a silver wedding band, but the other had a steady swing and patient
hands. I didn't return to that place for a long time, but knowing I could
mattered. Sometimes I drove to Harris Teeter after work,

filling the cart with a tub of yogurt, bag of pretzels,
a lone granola bar—my version of dinner if you did not cook.
I think I always knew one day I would have to live without you

yet for so long I feared motorcycle accident, plane crash,
freak heart attack. But hearts are not that complicated
and most of the time you can tell yours might be heading

toward disaster. I paid my toll. I paid for those behind me.
I told everyone we were fine, and I told myself Christmas
didn't matter, that we would celebrate sometime later.

The Laws of Less and More

I'm still thinking about what my tío said when I was twelve:
that I was chubby and needed to watch my weight.

Until then, my body had been meant
for only me.

Even decades later I am thinking of this seed he planted,
the soil I gave it, the sun of my belief.

I am thinking of what I did not eat for so long:
milk, cheese, peanut butter, bread, mayonnaise.

I did not eat a sandwich for so many years. I only yearned for
parts of me to disappear, for other parts

to show, be admired, render me beautiful. I believed
a body could do so much more if I gave it less.

Recently when I, in middle age, told my doctor I was gaining
weight despite no change in diet or exercise, she said, *you need to eat*

less. And now I think of all the lessons I learned when I was twelve
that I practiced for years—all the times I told myself *you should not have,*

you will not have, you should never, ever have. Restriction as devotion
became what others saw as *disciplined*, the only part of me I allowed to grow

wild.

The Last Holiday Party

A holiday party, your boss's house, somewhere in Durham.
You drove. You knew the way. We'd been there once before but still

I didn't know where we were going. You flicked on the radio
to NPR, sad songs and bits of bad news. I turned the heater vent

toward me, zipped my jacket all the way up. We had left no dog
at home, though you wanted one. I had said no, not now, maybe one day

but that was a year earlier or two, or somewhere back behind us,
a place no longer dotted on our map. Your boss had a dog,

a tiny scruffy thing, a Yorkie maybe, though I knew nothing
of breeds then, of how to pick, and you hadn't yet understood

you can't just leave a dog alone too long. You have to raise it
on rules of love. Love was a hard enough tug as it was.

The first holiday party that I had gone to at her place—a year earlier?
two?—she put the dog outside but made sure he wouldn't be cold,

cloaked him in a Christmas sweater, thick and woolly
and audaciously red. There he sat on the side stoop, waiting

for it all to be over: the guests, the hot cider, the wine bottles
and all those goblets, chunks of cheese and salty crackers,

carrot and celery sticks, a bowl of ranch dip. Your boss told us
the dog took antidepressants, and I wondered how he could be

that unhappy. What in the world did that dog want
that he did not have? You and I talked about this on the way home

that first time, that first party. We laughed, made jokes. You drove
and the road that night propelled us along its easy spine.

That last holiday party, you wanted to stay later than I did.
You handed me the keys. *Someone will give me a ride home*, you said

and it was late and I was too tired to argue. You had to tell me
how to get home. You had to say where to turn left, to turn

right, the signposts I might miss, that roundabout on Erwin Road.
You didn't tell me watch for deer, though I did, hidden behind

those shifting trees. The first time we went to that holiday party
at your boss's house, we peeked out at the side stoop before we left.

We got one last look at that dog. He had torn off his Christmas sweater.
It lay in a clump in stiff grass. He was cold, but he didn't want

to come in. That sweater, that dog, his silly conviction. For a long
time—so long that I lost track—we thought how very funny it all was.

Where Do You Get Your Ideas?

after Brendan Constantine

From a little church in my mind that sells little Bibles,
doesn't give them out for free (well, gives the not-as-nice ones,
the ones with plastic covers, not the gold-cover ones).
I don't buy either, but I go to the church

and pay for salvations, like a good idea
which is hard to find unless you know where to look
which is on Xenia Avenue at the Emporium
which specializes in lots and lots of wine, but buy the coffee
beans (that's what I do, before they're ground up),
open the bag, take a good whiff—that's where I got
one idea one time in this one life. In another life

I got an idea from a traveling musician pitching
a tent by the side of the road and busking for love
and romance and other dreamy things that he didn't really
want to play but they sounded so good when he strummed
them that I married him—yes! I did that!—and from him

I got many good ideas, though most are sad with burlap
blankets wrapped around their shoulders, their hands never
warm enough by the fire, but the fire seemed like a good idea
at the time, when it wasn't burning the roof, which was always.

Always is where I got another good idea, it's a storage facility
stuffed with all my memories and I return there more times than I want to—
I even have a cot set up in there! though I never sleep—
and I sort through waffle makers and glitter guns and the Hacky Sack
which is what I call my heart and there are many ideas stuck
like gum beneath tables and I find that if I work at it
long enough, they peel right off.

Hope Has Holes In Its Pockets

It's true what they say about jeans: they fit everyone but no one well.
They're comfortable but not flattering. They keep in the heat and also
trap the cold. Don't wear them skiing. Don't wear them hiking.
Don't wear them to a fancy restaurant, although now that might be
in fashion. If you're a farmer, forget what I said. You will love them
and hold them up with a big leather belt. You will bale hay in them.
You will brush the horses all while you wear your best blue jeans,
or your favorite, or your most broken in. Is there a difference? Sometimes

a heart needs breaking in. Sometimes it's better once it's been battered.
Sometimes the only way forward is to pull on those pants—jeans
made for everything, then. I didn't see them for what they were:
capable of being stitched and stretched and paired for any occasion.
Wear them with sneakers. Wear them with heels. Wear them with

rhinestones studded down their sides. Even when weary, they can be
washed and reborn—ready for the time of their life.

The Road of Love

There is a woman on the side of the road,
her car's one good tire embedded
with a nail deflating this rubber of lies.
She's traveled for miles

on roads her parents showed her
by corn fields, all stalks in straight rows,
through flat lands where she could spot
any town's church, its steeple

puncturing unknown horizon. And there was always,
somewhere in the distance, a red barn with a narrow door
where she supposed a farmer would emerge,
someone who knew the land and its

expectations, someone who could recite
the weather's recipes, who could sing
the hymn of seeds and sowing
and reaping. But now

she understands that no one emerges
from the red barn who knows
a damn thing, and out the wider barn door
bolt hungry goats and crying sheep

and chickens pecking ground for answers,
and wild dogs and feral cats who never stopped
scratching, and there she is,
that one wild horse, mane loose

because truth is this gallop
where no one needs a car made by man
and misunderstanding. Tell me
why we ever made rules

about whom to love. Tell the woman
the now-flat tire was never the good one, it was always
the others, the ones no one expected
to carry anything far, the ones who were rolling

forward all along.

You Are Not a Cat

You don't think you're so beautiful. You don't
preen. You don't expect to be the center
of the universe. You don't move slowly. You never
scratch things you aren't allowed to scratch.
(Is there something you're allowed to scratch?)
You don't ever saunter, or sun yourself—lying
in light with no cares in the world. You don't stay
out at night when you should be home. You don't
just disappear. After all, you have responsibilities
and expectations to meet—but you put them there,
didn't you?

You don't arch your back and hiss when you're
angry or scared, but sometimes you think that might be
easier. You have no claws, but sometimes you think
they'd come in handy. You don't know how to chase
and hunt, to catch and abolish, but on some days,
in some hours, you think maybe you could.

Grow

I can't remember the last time I slept well, so deeply I did not wake up until morning was meant for me. Maybe it was after one of B's parties at his little house on Greensboro Street when we would dance to 80's music. I brought a CD of my favorite songs, and we would all sway between windows and French doors, that passageway that led to his bedroom, a place I spent the night sometimes when we didn't know where we were going. I loved that house, though I never imagined living there. One story, brick fireplace, a kitchen big enough to feed a hunger but not big enough to concoct something too complicated. B asked me once to plant a garden for him, just outside the front door—the one we never used (we were always, all of us, going in and out the back door)—and I asked him for a budget, which he gave me (fifty dollars? one hundred?) and I bought beautiful possibilities like columbine and phlox and good dirt and I shoveled and pushed the plants into their new home. I didn't have a garden—he knew that—and back then I thought he asked me because he needed help with his landscape, a place that had not grown anything but weeds in years, but now I think he was trying to give me a piece of home in a town I never belonged to, that never belonged to me. He lived on a hill, so we could hear traffic—horns and tires and the sound of speed—but we were above it, a little cloud in a little sky. Pat Benatar, The Go-Go's, Michael Jackson—I miss the sound of their joy. I miss bowls of pretzels, someone pulling out a guitar, people sprawled on the floor, too tired to go home. None of us wanted to grow older, we all wanted to go back in some way or another, and we pushed off morning. B and I did that, for too long, probably. I wonder if columbine spreads its seed outside his door. I wonder if the good dirt made the bad dirt better. I wonder if phlox pushes from that earth every spring, refusing to grow elsewhere.

Hunger

You put on music, start up the stove, a flick of gas
and fire. I slice white potatoes, the staple of generations,
the thing that fills bellies, makes hunger flee
even if we can't stop craving.

You don't follow recipes, you select
based on instinct, meter out what you need
by eyeing it, by feel, by a taste I do not have.

All I have are yearnings.

You don't know me well enough to know the things
I want but do not have, or have but do not want, or wanted
but tossed out—onion skin, avocado pit,
what protects or keeps a fruit from rotting.

And what do I know of you? The thing you do not tell me
has a scent, nutty and strong. I don't ask for much,
not yet anyway. I watch in wonder at how you put together

a pile of odds and ends and make it into art. Then I wonder
when you will feed it to me, when you will take it all apart.

Dark Secret

I eat chocolate every morning. Not just a little.
I keep a clear plastic bin of bars in the pantry.
I buy bars when they're on sale

and when they're not, and when I say *buy*
I mean hoard. The bin has a blue latch I easily open.
Inside: dark chocolate, sea salt, the kind not popular

when I stopped eating it decades ago. I was a kid
who chucked Special Dark from my Halloween bag,
who favored the milk kind, who drank Swiss Miss every morning

until I was seventeen and the thing I loved stopped
loving me: acne, rashes, all the telltale signs my body should
stay the hell away. And now, after years of denial, this is what happens
when you let go of something or someone you know belongs to you:

a kindling of greed and desperation consume self-restraint.
I defined myself for years by how I followed rules,
never jumped no-trespassing fences, kept my promises

and met deadlines, denied for so long all the ways my body
wanted to devour and be devoured. So I am left now
with a bin, and I eat the bars, not even slowly,

and with no apology.

Confession

after a line by Reginald Dwayne Betts

A confession begins in the doorframe of your house.
Outside, the cold is wet with knowing, the street bereft of cars.
You love me but can't be with me—these your words like gravel
that cannot mound into more than an alley behind the backs of houses.

A confession begins with a slam of car door, a key, an engine,
the exhausted night through this windshield I have looked through
a hundred times but never seen such limp stars, and that moon
like a white fist without a face.

I cannot leave and I cannot stay. I cannot love you but I can't
unlove you. I can't find the words to this confession
because what I want would become a thirst
even a desert could not know.

A confession begins in the doorframe of your house.
I am standing in your cold and sleepless night. You open the door
the way you always do, unable to tell me to go, unable to be with me
but unable to stop yourself from saying come in.

Places I Looked for You

after Natalie Kusz

In every airport, at the last gate, in a plastic chair,
your head lowered, reading an article I might never understand,
or writing one, having the terminology for everything but *stay*

On side streets, especially in rain, pedaling a bike,
your yellow poncho flapping, like applause, like surprise,
like a bloom defying gray

In any soybean field, between rows of yesterday
and what might have been, standing in boots flecked
with hard day's dirt and the smear of regret

In every small city, in any blue truck
or back bedroom tinged with the day's last
drunken light that can soften and forget

At night, in dreams, never the same one, but always
we were young and we lay side by side like matchsticks
in a box, ready for the troubled flame

And I don't need to find you, not anymore,
but I know I will see you just once—in a crowd, on a train,
in a long line—and I wonder if I will know by then

the language for *I'm sorry*, for *goodbye*

What to Look for in a Cabbage

A head that is firm and heavy for its size,
but not too big. No blemishes, only a sheen
to the leaves. Crisp rather than tender. Sharp green

or mahogany red, a color wedded to disaster.
If you pick right, the cabbage can be easily sliced open,
turned into slaw or boiled in stew, sautéed
into softness. All you need is imagination

and a belief in selecting the vegetable so many others
ignored, going instead for white potatoes,
iceberg lettuce, cucumbers, none of which will ever offer
the same nutrition as a cruciferous, or the same love
as the one so often passed over.

Cabbage picked after a frost will be sweeter
than before. Ask the farmer, ask the woman standing
with a straw hat in front of a makeshift table filled
with a hundred cabbage heads, ask anyone who will answer

what this cabbage has endured.

It's a Doggy-Dog World

So many people don't hear dog-eat-dog because who wants
to think about one animal consuming another? We get it wrong,
we think we can care less but really we could not. And which one of us
wouldn't prefer tender hooks to tenterhooks? Who doesn't want to believe
tenderness, even in a hook, is possible?

People hold on to what they want to hear.
They pull out the smallest part of a lie or a *maybe*
and make it big, and soon it's a tent large enough
to block out bearing-down truth. Once,

a radiologist looked at my films and told me
that dot—*see that dot?*—had an 85% chance
of being cancer. What did I hear? Fifteen percent
chance of being nothing, and I told myself fifteen was more
than ten and more than five and way more than zero.
I plugged my ears, said la-la-la
then juggled so I didn't have to hold tight
to a number that could defeat me,
so I didn't have to see

a dog eating another dog,
a dog that could be me.

How to Be Beautiful

Forget what everyone said when you were dark-haired
with smooth olive skin, slender arms, strong legs.

Life takes everyone's little pretties, slowly or quickly.
You used to turn heads, catch whistles, receive secret

messages and love letters from men too old, too young,
too married, too angry, too unattached, too busy, too

unimaginative to understand your beauty was never
in your face. Your hair is turning silver now like the underside

of maple leaves. You still have strong legs but now you could give
a rat's ass about stockings, high heels. It's sneakers for you,

shoes your mother called clunks. You are happiest in T-shirts
and sport shorts and you still run every Wednesday morning

before the day has begun, when it is dark and you can forget
what people thought of you, what they think now,

because you feel the muscles in your legs
which are stronger like everything else about you.

Your day began a couple of decades ago, which is why
darkness doesn't scare you. You feel sorry for the girls

who wait at the bus stop, bags of youth heavy
on their backs. You run past, faster now, not in speed

but in the way you know how to look forward, not back,
how to stop all that yearning for something

you only briefly had.

OBIT: Good Girlfriend

after Victoria Chang

Good girlfriend: died on August 17, 1996, and again
November 27, 2001. Such sudden deaths. The first
in a gymnasium filled with colleagues—
witnesses, onlookers, gawkers (what happens
when you mix passion and wages like a bad drink).
Let's call that one a heart

attack. The next in her own home
unable to be stopped though she saw it
coming. Humiliation beats its wings
through broken windows.

People say what everyone says
about the dead: *she lit up a room*, but that
was before. Now it's whispered. Now
she flicks on a lighter, burns
the curtains, clothes,
curly hair of every lover.

In the morning she rolls up the blinds, squints at the light.
It hurts, all this shiny-like-sequins sky, but she stares at it
anyway, fumbling for sunglasses, knowing they won't help
this splitting headache she will never be rid of again.

Kindness. Caring. Empathy.
She didn't know what they could buy
until now that they've expired

and some part of her cares
but some part of her gets that she is
better off like this

with her punching bag attitude
and this ashtray heart.

Persuasion in the Form Of

after Destiny O. Birdsong

Shuly you have a nice
Shuly you have a hot
Shuly you have an amazing
Shuly I just want
Shuly can we
Shuly why aren't we
Shuly when will we
Shuly you are too
Shuly I didn't mean
Shuly you take everything I say and
Shuly I just want
Shuly I just need
Shuly I'm so
Shuly please say you
Shuly I don't need
Shuly let's get
Shuly I would never ask if I knew right now you
Shuly let's just see what
Shuly I didn't mean it like
Shuly you take everything I say and
Shuly I just want
Shuly I just need
Shuly you never
Shuly I feel like you're being a whiny little
Shuly why can't you
Shuly you are so
Shuly you are too
Shuly you really are
Shuly I told you that
Shuly I never said
Shuly don't be like
Shuly I meant every word I

You Are Not a Dog

You do not bark when strangers get too close.
You do not expect others to clean up your mess.
You do not shed. (Okay, you shed a little.) (A lot.)

You do not expect a treat every time you do
what someone asks you to. You do not growl
at the meanies standing at the edge of their yards,
one zap away from breaking out.

You don't live in the moment. You don't wag your tail
all the time. You don't feel satisfied when you've gotten stinky.
You don't feel glee when you overeat.

You do not stick your head out the car window
or wake everyone up just because you're hungry.
You do not scratch in public, sniff your secret places,
or poop in other people's yards.

You, you, you do not test the fences
other people put up to keep you out
or keep you in. You don't keep digging
when someone yells at you to stop.
You don't refuse to budge
when people tell you

you are too much in the way.

Joy

Up on a rooftop restaurant at the corner of Franklin and Airport Roads,
the streetlight stopping and starting the cars below,
I drank more than I'd ever drunk before. I was leaving a job
I had loved so long, a job that had loved me through my marriage
and divorce, through days when my face was swollen with grief,

a job that had combed my hair when I could not,
a job that never said *have you considered makeup* or
did you look in the mirror before saying yes to that outfit,
a job that said *sure* when I declared I was going to Winston-Salem
every Tuesday night to dance and would not get home until
it was so late the highways would be empty save for truckers,
and by the way I won't be in to work until ten the next morning,
a job that said *as long as you come back*

and I always did
until that November

when I said I'm bored, I need a change,
I don't think I can do this anymore.

Up on a rooftop restaurant, the chilled air
made its way around the tables, and I flirted with strangers
while my friends toasted my next step
except I didn't know what was next.

Talking to no one was a man I had invited
who would never love me

and I was free finally, and isn't this what I wanted,
isn't this what I asked for, when I said, I have to go?

Joy was in the streetlight on the corner of Franklin and Airport Roads
turning green yellow red and back again
and it seemed so close up there on that
rooftop
restaurant
close enough that if I leaned
over the edge, I could almost touch it
except once I leaned
I understood how far away
it really was.

Your Story Here

I want to tell you a story.

I want to tell you a story with no end.

A story with a temper but a side of fruit.

A story with a stutter, a sneeze, a slow burn.

I want to tell you a story with lips and hips and a neck
brace. A story with wisdom teeth and a bar of chocolate
in its pocket and tricks and jacks and possibly an ax
up its sleeve.

A story with a trash can and torn raft and cracked
coffee mug, with a blue bowl of freshly washed kale.

What I mean is

a story that's saintly but with secrets: the binge-
watch of a bad series, a little weed, an affair
that according to the story is over but never
is. I want to tell you a story with flip

flops and tongs and that one trip to Texas when everyone
drank too much tequila and no one paid the taxi driver and that one time
with the trapeze that everyone says couldn't possibly have happened
but everyone still believes.

A story with no name but with a little black book. A story
with no address but with plenty of postcards from women seeking
apologies and from kids who still believe in Santa. A story

with an alley, a yellow galley kitchen, a pocketknife and wind chimes
that sway on summer nights, no longer waiting to be asked to dance.

A story with a heart murmur and strong legs, a bean bag chair
and an old Polaroid, a snow blower and a rodeo-worthy *sombrero*.

A story that comes with french fries and an opened gate
and a pond protected by a thousand
cattails.

I want to tell you a story.

A story with no shame.

A story with a seventh inning. And broken glass. A steel bridge
and an addiction. With a bandana, bikini, Birkenstocks.

I want to tell you a story.

I want to tell you.

With a lighter, a lashing out,
a last kiss.

He and I Haven't Spoken in Years

Surely they have children together, though it's true I don't want
to see pictures, don't need to know ages or achievements. I'll let
them have a cat but not a dog. I'll let them have Disney but not
European vacations. I don't need to know her name or how they
met. I don't want to know if her cooking made him soft, or her
kindness made him patient. I don't want to know if he grew a
beard or lost his hair. He stands straight for me still, his face free
of creases. He still runs marathons, swims across lakes, shovels
long driveways of snow. Still believes in big back porches, the
bite of jalapeños, making clean breaks. Surely she believes in
homemade jam, the hum of overhead fans, and conviction over
curiosity. Surely she rubs his shoulders while standing behind him
at the kitchen table, the pine one his mother insisted he inherit
despite its hobbled leg and scratched surface. Surely the kids argue
about who has to feed the chickens, sweep the barn floor, scrub
the basin in the washroom. So many things to keep clean. Surely
she can't keep up with it all, makes a chores list, crosses it out
but never finishes. Life out there—surely they live *out there* where
there are dirt stretches and welded wire fences to fend off foxes—
means an endless mending of pants, darning socks, stitching cuts.
Surely she has no time to gaze out the window of her husband's
heart, to ask about its former tenants. Surely he never thinks of
me, not even when the moonlight has no place to hide, or the fox
digs a hole, or the barn door swings open accidentally on nights
when no one latched it right.

Wife

The word, so close to the word life,
which is what you are supposed to vow in terms of time.

The first time I married—already there I am telling
you this is doomed—I had just turned twenty-nine,

an unseasoned age still, for I did not understand
that marital love was green-stemmed, slight, piping

its way toward improbable sky, capable of death
due to frost, trample, insect destruction,

the toss of old dice. I went on to love but
not be loved, to work hard but

not be praised, to buy a house but not be warm,
yet love found me in its other forms:

colleagues, family members, fellow dancers,
friends of friends of friends.

I was not a wife for long and the truth is
I was never a good one. I wanted more than I could

afford to give. I hid truths and offered smiles. I loved
but maybe in none of the right places,

none of the right ways, and I thought I wanted to be
his wife, but then he left, which was three and a half years

later in a Chevy with a lamp I did not need in the backseat,
but with a title I believed I did. So much later, I discovered

this: a small and tender stalk, and though it would not grow
for eight more years, I kept it safe

from insect destruction, trample,
and any kind of frost.

The End of the Season

In March, just before flowers broke
into white blossoms, he started to limp,
his left hind leg giving out.

We stood side by side at the kitchen window
to witness the step, step, stumble, step, step,
stumble. Is it time, one of us asked. Step, step,

stumble. How will we know when it's the right time,
we had asked our vet the year before, when he had begun
pacing outside the doggy door, unable to recall

how to press his muzzle against it and return inside
to us. Make a list, our vet said, of three to five things
that make his life a good one, and when most of the list is gone,

you'll know.

Running, walking, eating,
holding his bladder and bowels.

The summer before, we had taken him to the city pool
on the day they let all dogs, for five bucks, jump in
before the pool got cleaned and drained for the end

of the season, and we had snapped him into a green life
jacket, and he had taken a run and leapt
into the still-warm water and paddled

as if he were not tired and deaf and toothless.
We stood side by side at the edge
of the pool. We let him swim
until there was no one else left.

It's a small thing in life, a dog, is it not?

He was peeing in the house more and more
but we cleaned it up, said he could still hold on.
Until that March day of his step, step, stumble.

Small is relative. A fourteen-pound animal eclipses
an insect. From high up, a giant sequoia, an Appalachian
Mountain, a Great Lake might seem impossibly small.

I packed a bag of biscuits for that last
trip to the vet. I sat on the floor with him
out in the lobby, waiting for his name and ours

to be called. I fed Barney biscuit after biscuit
and still there were more
and for a moment it seemed possible

we might never run out.

You Worry Too Much

You worry like it's an all-you-can-eat buffet. You worry like
it's a first love: unforgettable, hard to shake. You worry like
it's a master class you've paid good money to take so you can't
quit now but sometimes you wonder who's the master. You worry

like it's a march for equality: teeny and big worries parade together
into your hamster-wheel brain. You worry about which flight to take,
what hour to leave, whether the trip is too long or too short,
so what date should you go? *Just pick one*, your husband says.
He knows how things can change but if you don't try something
you'll try nothing. He knows sometimes you want to try nothing.
You worry about cell phone addiction and the recycling bin piled up
with single-use plastics and the water spurting too long from the faucet
when anyone washes their hands, if they even wash their hands,
why can't people just wash their hands? You worry about

your parents and their slowing days, your own slowing days,
the pill you have to take at night. You worry one day it will be two
or three, or that nothing will work, that one day you won't sleep.
Just take the pill, your husband says. *If it stops working,
you'll deal with it then.* His stairs of logic to your turnstile of worry.

You worry about the neighbor's lost dog never coming home.
You worry that someone will steal your dog even though you never
leave her outside if you aren't there to glance out the kitchen window
every two seconds. You worry when you leave the house
she won't be okay because mostly she isn't although your husband says
mostly she is and he's probably right because he's a half-full
kind of person and you've always been half-empty—no, empty-empty,
a pit below the glass sucking all the water out. He says *you can't worry
about the dog having a bad day every once in a while. She'll be fine.*

He means you'll be fine. He means get your act together but he's too nice
to say that. He rubs your back. He fixes all the things you don't
worry about because you didn't even know they needed fixing:
the drain letting go of water too slowly, the pipe begging for stuffing
around its edges, the branch desperate to be sawed off.
You wonder about what else needs fixing, besides you.

You want to know what will happen and when and for how long
and mostly the cost. You read the end of the book before you've begun.
You count how many rows to reach the exit window. You take your pill
every night and still you forget that if nothing good lasts forever
that also means nothing bad will.

Soft-Boiled Eggs on Any Morning

They say a watched pot never boils
but I've stood over plenty and they always do
if I wait long enough, which I was raised to do.

To get an egg to turn soft-boiled—as opposed
to hard—so the yolk can still leak
out, not having toughened yet,

you must start with eggs in cold water
and heat them over flame in a pot
gifted to you by the aunt

who never liked you, maybe even
never loved you, yet she gave you this pot
which has endured your bad marriage,

your bout with cancer, the death of your friend
who took your hands in hers and said
it's time to dye your hair

because she promised to tell you
when the strands were too peppered, and though
you no longer dye anything

now that she is dead, you ache for her hands
and for the smooth and scarless skin
on your chest and for the way you once

believed love was enough. Now you stand
beside the stove and watch the water boil—
it always does, it always will—

and once this bath splashes against
the sides of this silver, sturdy pot,
you set the timer, two and a half minutes long

and wait for it to be over. Anyone
can wait those minutes. The eggs clink
against each other. Steam rises

toward your face and finds it.

Notes on Nostalgia

1.

The dogwood breaks open its white petals. Soon rain will stain them brown.

2.

When rain comes, which it does nearly every afternoon, it exhausts itself on my windows.

3.

My mother told me, *I will always be near you.* I try to believe her the way I try to believe I am good and things will turn out fine. But look, a bird has bashed into the bay window and flails now in the mulch below. What pitiful wings we all have.

4.

My dog snores in the bed beside me. Her sleep reminds me of that time I left someone I loved not because I wanted to but because I knew I should. That was a time I could not breathe well. That was a time when I lost my ability to sing.

5.

If I start out telling you I'm about to cry, maybe that will quench this sad sort of thirst.

6.

There's an art to goodbye, though it took me many years to recognize that one could groom this talent, could become skilled and beastly on stage, could draw crowds. But no one applauds me, for I am still at the stick-figure stage. I let go of nothing, except rusted canning jar lids and old ChapStick, and even those I keep too long.

7.

I miss my mother, though I saw her days ago. She has not called today, and I have spent my morning wondering how I will manage when she never says *where are you* again.

8.

The humidity outside is thick, like ChapStick, except no one wants to wear it. Loss is that way too. Unless, of course, you're losing the bad shit.

9.

A dog teaches you to pick it all up, no matter how awful it smells, no matter its lack of solidity. I know you don't want to picture this, but this is what it's like for me to imagine impending loss every day.

10.

See this pink napkin? My mother made it for me. She knew, God she always knew, I would have so much to clean up.

On the Day My Bridal Dress Goes to Goodwill

I kept it twenty-two years in my childhood closet,
shoving it aside when I visited my parents
to make room for a purple hoodie, a long-sleeved
blue sweater, a pair of jeans
folded on a metal hanger. I wanted the dress

to go to someone young I would surely find
who could not yet afford a fancy frock,
who could not afford lace edgings
or capped sleeves, who could not afford

to divorce because surely someone else
would have better luck in that dress if I just found
the right person. But anyone knows that luck

is what you get when you stop looking, when you stumble
upon it on the far side of a thrift store rack
hanging there as if it has nowhere to go but home

with you, as if it's been waiting all along,
tucked into a plastic bag that knows how to zip
up its secrets. Luck is almost the same
thing as hope, just a little less shiny,
a little less white.

We Writers

after Rebecca Elson

We are shepherds, bartenders,
beauticians. We are chefs
of tender meats.

We know how to knot, how to plot
the personal, how to search and rescue.
We know how to die
a hundred deaths
and still lie.

There is nothing we can't
hook onto the end of a line
and fling into fresh water
that won't retrieve
a wriggling,
shimmering belief.

But sometimes this crowded world
feels lonely with its mistakes,
missed connections, miscarriages
of the heart.

Sometimes truths are animals
no one thinks to feed.

Your Goodness or Mine

after a line from Matthew Olzmann

No longer satisfied with the way fairness works, I want to build a
scale that weighs your goodness against mine. Come, everyone stand
on it, take your turn, tell me what your generosity is worth and how
it compares to Antonio's, Elijah's, Marisol's, and to Guadalupe, who
bathed her mother this morning with a new pink sponge and then dried
her papery skin with a terrycloth towel, just laundered, and lent her arm
for balance as her mother tottered one leg at a time into loose pants with
an unraveling drawstring. Did you do something good today, and how
much did it weigh and for what price? Is it better than what Guadalupe
did, or Samuel who opened the door for a young woman loaded with
plastic grocery bags in her arms? Was his single act worth anything
since the woman was beautiful and as she struggled through the door he
admired the roundness of her body in all the right places? And her plastic
bags most likely won't be recycled, will outlive us all, so is it good, this
small act of kindness, when maybe the better thing would have been for
him to hold the door shut and tell her to use paper? And what about
Patricia who is now taking a call in her cubicle from a disgruntled
customer, she is saying, "Uh-huh, uh-huh," when what she really wants
is to tell him he's a prick for yelling at her, but she is kind today, unlike
the other days when she hangs up on customers who call her bitch, idiot,
a useless piece of *. Does her goodness today weigh a little more because
it's unusual and because the customer is particularly nasty and Patricia
has a son to feed and rent to pay, rent that is high because she wants her
baby, her Felipe, to go to a school in this district with its parents who
love a good fundraiser and have demanded all kids have an iPad, and
isn't Patricia good to care about her son though she hates the parents
who pat her on the hand and tell her she doesn't have to bake cookies
for the sale, they say they know, she has too much to do, they will take
care of it, they will bake an extra pan of brownies for her, but instead
Patricia wakes early on Saturday to stir coconut with chocolate chips
into flour and butter and roll it all into balls and place them on a baking
sheet in rows like the crops her father planted, like the life she once
knew and gave up for this, for Felipe?

Tell me is your goodness heavier, worth more in this balance and barter of life than that of this person or that one, and does it mean you deserve more? And aren't we all, some days, the prick on the phone who yells because he cannot see Patricia standing at the bake sale along with all the other parents, holding out her tray filled with cookies, so many cookies, that will be the first to get bought?

Stupid People

So many people are stupid. I've resigned myself
to this for some time now. Stupid people blame
other people for the things they don't want to know.
They blame the wind for rain they squeezed from clouds.
They blame the sun for their having to squint instead of
turning and walking away.

Stupid people have lost things: power, money, respect.
Or they long for these things or something else they can't bear
to admit or name. They stumble toward everything they want and break jars,
bottles, ladders, lives on their way toward their stupid, unkempt dreams.

But now I smell the wind's whistle through the Leyland cypress in my yard,
and the rain, once so many miles away, clatters now
onto the pale blue deck someone built for me with steady hands
seven summers ago, and seven summers before that,
I did not know a thing about a Leyland cypress,

I only knew *evergreens*, that generic, all-encompassing
name that specifies nothing, that boxes everything into one category
and shrugs with ignorance. I remember those years where I followed
my stupid heart down so many roads I forgot which was east
and west and I journeyed over rocks I should have recognized
for their sharpness, their ability to be thrown

through a window. My window. I blamed the wind.
I said it could pick up gravel and toss it like confetti.
But I was the party maker, the vandal, the stumbling
stupid person with her hand raised in the air, ready to fling,
willing to break anything while longing for nothing
but love.

I Look for Donna Every Time

Donna takes the returned items—*Party Size!*
Ruffles and a jar of honey—from the guy in front of me
at Kroger and gives him back cash.   Donna takes my
discards—two bottles of Vitamin D gummies—and gives me
all my credit card money.   Donna helps the cashier in lane five
to hustle the conveyor belt of groceries: hamburger buns, spicy
mustard, mayo, two kinds of cheddar cheese.   Donna keeps
the rainbow ice cream from melting, plopping it into two plastic bags.
Donna's always there. Donna never frowns. Donna ever says okay.
               Donna   will you help me?
Donna makes the beeping sounds go away in the self-checkout lines.
Donna keys in the codes and says now you should be fine.

Letter to the Children of the Future

You can't see the blue bird box out my window.
I don't know whether this blue bird box will exist,
or any bird boxes, or any birds. I want to tell you
to believe in them, but you might not know what I mean,
so let me start here: a bird can be small and light,
with beak and wings, feathers and clawed feet. A little
beating heart, eyes that do not blink. Birds build nests
in branches and bushes, in gutters and eaves.
I'd like to think a bird can build a nest anywhere,
taking fallen twig and bits of string, discarded
pieces, soft and hard pieces, things that can bend
and be given new life.

I want to tell you to be a bird, but you might not know
what it means to fly. You might not have wings.
You might not know what words can build
soft places in the world. You might not know
how to sing.

What It Takes

The sun does not rise easily. A whole planet must spin
on its axis—take with it warring countries, pull culture
clashes and opposing ideologies round and round—to make

these days begin. The colors, not simple either—all splotches of red
and orange and another hue so hard to name I only know
it's bold enough to smear the sky.

There's a reason such audacious colors strip the heavens
of nightly blue elegance. Boldness requires space
and freedom and takes it all upon morning.

Do you have what it takes? You must,
for you're a girl and no one will hand it
over, just like that. Be the rising sun. Be

the hue I cannot name.

This Is the Poem I Did Not Write

while snapping off branches, hauling brush
to the curb. Searching for my car keys, losing
my belief in certainty. Slicing lemons for a party
I don't want to have, holding the door open & saying
polite things I've been taught to offer. Hitchhiking
through relationships. Running so my heart won't
give up. Trashing old makeup I never
learned to use. Cutting a brownie in two
knowing I will eat both halves
for breakfast. A call to my mother, first
and last thing I do.

after Rita Dove

Anyway

after Mary Oliver

1.

The garter snake disappears in the St. John's wort
outside my door, the canopy of elliptical leaves
the perfect place
to hide and gulp and burrow.

There are days when I, too, want a place
where no one thinks to look,
where what reaches me is only
lazy heat, tickle of grass,
elastic hours—
not news, not aches,
not this brevity.

2.

Find joy in peeling the orange.
Seek a cold creek and stand in its grace.
Walk through forest and understand how it breathes,
which is not through greed. Trees listen and lend,
they bend
with the hardest
wind.

3.

Today, rain seeps through a hole in the sky
and we take cover under a red awning,
waiting it out—

what you choose
when you can do
nothing else.

The dog shakes and hunkers down
behind us, unaware
this weather
will soon end.

4.

Fear is a potion
I drank my whole life.

There was no magic
in this elixir.

The magic was always
in the miracle
of one more day.

Even the hard ones
offered me stones
to throw
at my anxiety.

5.

What I loved in the beginning was possibility.
Now, I see doors closing: one here, another there.
People think I mean despair, but fewer choices
make selection simpler.

6.

Sometimes, I admit, I miss the youth
I held in my hands like a lamp. How far
I could see. I did not think about how long
the light would last, or I thought about it
but somehow believed it would anyway.

Anyway was a word I ate my whole life,
but now it tastes sweeter
because it arrives so seldom.

7.

In the gold coin of what I offer, there is no
value other than what you will buy with this.
Even now, in the market of our lives,
there is always an exchange. You cannot
keep all the gold coins and not suffer with poverty.

I will not tell you give it all away,
but give most, more than you want.
You'll see—it comes back, but not in the way
you think

the same way your face
becomes that of someone else,
later, in the mirror.

You glimpse possibility
anyway.

A Working Definition of *Yes*

It's your ruffled, red dress. It's an investment in hope, expecting
more over less. It's the arrest of a villain. It's the chest of drawers
that stores your faded blue dreams. It's a canopy of aspen trees,
and a gate with a broken latch. It's the hatching of eggs and the
mess of dirty dishes you leave in a heap. It's a leap of faith, the
stray you take in, the wind in your hair on a hike on the edge of
some rock at the end of hard days. It's the fraying of your doubts.
It's staying when it's easier to get going. It's the knowing flame that
warms your coldest hand. Yes is rarely bland. It's the band that
plays late into night and hopes to catch a break. It's waking up.
It's an offer. It's more like cash than credit, more like the unedited
version, more like on the verge than on the fence. Yes is your best
back pocket. It's a locket with your own hair. Yes is everywhere—
like fireflies and silver-sided leaves and dogs that chase the rain.
Like dandelion seeds blowing in summer's backyard. Like all
those stars behind every cloud you ever saw. Yes is without regret,
without regard.

Poem in Which I Fail to Teach My Dog How to Fetch

after Laura Passin

I throw the tennis ball. She chases it, grabs it in her mouth, sprints as far from me as possible in our fenced-in yard. She plops down beneath a Leyland cypress. The day is filled with opposites: moist mulch and dry grass, broken branch and whole-hearted effort. *Here*, I call. I am using the sweet voice the vet psychiatrist told me to, not the *hell no* one I prefer. *Here*, I call again. I use the hand signal, my right palm facing me, beckoning from air to flat against my chest. In my left hand, a chicken-flavored treat. My dog holds the ball in her mouth, blinks at me. *Uh-oh*, I say. *Uh-oh* is our neutralizing word, the word the trainer said to use when the dog ignores your command. You're not supposed to keep repeating the command or else the dog learns only to respond after the third or fourth of fifth time. Or in my case: never. *Here*, I say, do the hand signal, offer the treat. *Who wants a treat?* Already I have resorted to pleading. The day is long in light, short in reply. When my husband first brought her home, when she was fourteen weeks old, I was so overwhelmed by her wildness, whimpers, ignorance of rules that I had a meltdown on our corduroy couch. *One day you'll love her*, he said. *How do you know*, I asked. *I know*, he said, *because I know you*. He settled onto the couch beside me, held me in his arms. That saying about love being patient, I suppose it's true. *Here*, I say, and the day, like any other, fills with light and shadow, weed and flower. *Uh-oh*, I say. *Here*, I say. She stares at me. You don't always get a choice about what life brings, what it does not. She spots a squirrel, darts after it, leaves behind the ball that now no one will retrieve. There are a hundred lessons she must be trying to teach me, and I have hardly mastered one.

From Up in Space

Light matters less, and the weight of things
changes. It's why I came. A pound of grief might become
an ounce, might float like droplets poised with nowhere to go.

I understand what will happen once I'm back
on ground, when the rocket ship blasts its last billow of smoke
like a cape incapable of staving off my drop down

to what I know: you are going to leave me
in some amount of time. I had hoped to make it longer
all the hours I remained up there, but I understand now

I did not, like so many other things I could not stop.

Some Kind of Prayer

What can I tell you that you do not already know?
Listen to the grass, its long legs whistling as it swishes.
Touch the brush of cattails, the brittle wings of pine cones,
the dry skin of chokeberries—feel
their burst. Taste rain. Say you're sorry

not for what you did but for how you doubted
yourself for so long. This life is filled
with a million cocoons and you can choose
how long, which one, or none.

Sleep is so close. Run now, run.

Personal Acknowledgments

A book is never made without the help of many people, so here I give a big thank you to:

Emily Fine, for trading writing with me weekly for more than a little while now, and who is always willing to give me feedback on my work. Girl, you've been with me since the Dark Ages, and we still have miles to go.

My writer friends Peggy Heitmann, padumachitta, Lois Anne, Susan Brazas Goldberg, and Martha Pedersen, for trading writing prompts with me and helping usher poems onto the page.

Seema Reza (and CBAW), for showing me how to better trust my writing instincts.

My Tuesday Let's Write Together class. Because I try out my own writing prompts before giving them to you in class, I have gotten a lot of poetry written because of you. You all so often inspire me and keep me going in difficult times. You are the highlight of my every week.

Carla Sameth, Courtney LeBlanc, and Laura Lee Washburn, for their thoughtful words on the back cover of this book.

My wonderful parents, for always believing in me and helping me believe in myself. You will always have my heart. I appreciate that you still get excited when your adult daughter accomplishes even the most minor thing.

My sister, Romy, for the loving support. You always rejoice at my successes and want me to shine.

My husband, Preston, for wanting my dreams to come true. You don't always "get" poetry, but you get my love for it, and you love me, so you cheer me on and ensure I have the time and space to write.

My dog, Kibbi, who brought many hard and wonderful gifts to me in her lifetime. I miss your silly ways.

Kevin Morgan Watson and Press 53, for bringing this book into the world. And since one sentence is not enough to say what I need to say about this publisher, here are some more: Years ago, I met Kevin at a writing conference. Years later, I reached out to him for advice and he took time out of his busy work to talk to me and help me. Years later, Press 53 published my debut story collection. I suspected I would love working with Kevin and his small press, and I was right. He and I have been working together ever since—teaming up to bring workshops to writers around the country and the globe. Kevin is always generous, fair, and big-hearted. (Also, he always makes me laugh.) I didn't know if Press 53 would want to publish my second poetry collection, but I was fortunate: Christopher Forrest, Press 53's poetry editor, said yes to my manuscript. He's been a wonderful editor, and I want to thank him here. And for you, Kevin Morgan Watson, I got more words: Thank you for building a press that is a dream publisher. Thank you for the kindness that you bring to the work. Thank you for all you do, and, most importantly, thank you for being fabulous you.

Inspirations and Borrowings Explained

"Anyway": This poem borrowed the style of "To Begin With, The Sweet Grass" by Mary Oliver.

"Confession,": I borrowed the words "A confessions begins" from the first line of the poem "Parking Lot" by Reginald Dwayne Betts.

"OBIT: Good Girlfriend": The title and idea and style were inspired by and borrowed from the many "Obit" poems by Victoria Chang.

"Persuasion In the Form Of": This poem borrowed the style of Destiny O. Birdsong's poem "Bandwidth."

"Places I Looked for You": The style was borrowed from Natalie Kusz's essay "Now and Then I Look for You," and her title inspired mine.

"Poem in Which I Fail to Teach My Dog How to Fetch": The title was inspired by the title of the poem "Poem in which I Fail to Teach Homer" by Laura Passin.

"Practicing": The title was borrowed from and the idea was inspired by the poem "Practicing" by Ciona Rouse.

"Starter Marriage": This poem borrowed the style of Erin Adair-Hodges' poem "Portrait of Mother: 1985" as well as the words "First there was the word and the word was" from the first line.

"This Is the Poem I Did Not Write": This poem borrowed the title and style from "This Is the Poem I Did Not Write" by Rita Dove.

"We Writers": The title and style were borrowed from Rebecca Elson's "We Astronomers."

"What I Mean When I Say Agronomist": The title was borrowed from and the idea was inspired by the the many Geffrey Davis "What I Mean When I Say . . ." poems.

"What to Look for in a Cabbage": The title was inspired by the title of the poem "What To Look For In A Horse" by Brett Elizabeth Jenkins.

"Where Do You Get Your Ideas?": The title and idea were inspired by and borrowed from the poem "Where Do You Get Your Ideas?" by Brendan Constantine.

"Your Goodness or Mine": This poem borrowed the words "No longer satisfied" from the first line of Matthew Olzmann's poem "Build, Now, a Monument."

Shuly Xóchitl Cawood is the author of several books, including *A Small Thing to Want: Stories* (Press 53), the poetry collection *Trouble Can Be So Beautiful at the Beginning*, winner of the Adrienne Bond Award for Poetry (Mercer University Press), and the flash essay collection *What the Fortune Teller Would Have Said*, winner of the Iron Horse Literary Review Prose Chapbook Competition (Texas Tech University Press). Originally from Ohio, Shuly currently lives in East Tennessee. She has an MFA in creative writing from Queens University of Charlotte, and she loves leading writing workshops, hiking in the woods, and eating dark chocolate. Learn more about her at shulycawood.com

Printed in the USA
CPSIA information can be obtained
at www.ICGtesting.com
JSHW020944010923
47376JS00001B/59